I0815914

You Can't Have It All

You Can't Have It All

A POEM BY

Barbara Ras

PAINTINGS BY

Terrell James

TRINITY UNIVERSITY PRESS
San Antonio, Texas

Barbara Ras, Terrell James, and Trinity University Press gratefully acknowledge Sarah Fitzsimons for her generous support of the publication of *You Can't Have It All*.

You Can't Have It All

You Can't Have It All

But you can have the fig tree and its fat leaves like clown hands

gloved with green. You can have the touch of a single eleven-year-old
finger

on your cheek, waking you at one a.m. to say the hamster is back.

You can have the purr of the cat and the soulful look
of the black dog, the look that says, If I could I would bite
every sorrow until it fled,

and when it is August,

you can have it August and abundantly so. You can have love,

though often it will be mysterious,

like the white foam

that bubbles up at the top of the bean pot over the red kidneys

until you realize foam's twin is blood.

You can have the skin at the center between a man's legs,

so solid, so doll-like. You can have the life of the mind,

glowing occasionally in priestly vestments,

never admitting pettiness,

never stooping to bribe the sullen guard who'll tell you

all roads narrow at the border.

You can speak a foreign language, sometimes,

and it can mean something. You can visit the marker on the grave

where your father wept openly.

You can't bring back the dead,

but you can have the words *forgive* and *forget* hold hands

as if they meant to spend a lifetime together.

And you can be grateful

for makeup, the way it kisses your face, half spice, half amnesia, grateful

for Mozart, his many notes racing one another towards joy, for towels

sucking up the drops on your clean skin, and for deeper thirsts,

for passion fruit, for saliva.

You can have the dream,

the dream of Egypt, the horses of Egypt and you riding in the hot sand.

You can have your grandfather sitting on the side of your bed,

at least for a while,

you can have clouds and letters, the leaping

of distances, and Indian food with yellow sauce like sunrise.

You can't count on grace to pick you out of a crowd

but here is your friend to teach you how to high jump,

how to throw yourself over the bar, backwards,

until you learn about love, about sweet surrender,

and here are periwinkles, buses that kneel, farms in the mind

as real as Africa.

And when adulthood fails you,

you can still summon the memory of the black swan on the pond

of your childhood,

the rye bread with peanut butter and bananas

your grandmother gave you while the rest of the family slept.

There is the voice you can still summon at will, like your mother's,

it will always whisper, you can't have it all,

but there is this.

About the Poem

In a phone call some years ago that Barbara Ras had with her friend Brooke Williams, the two waxed philosophically about the idea "you can't have it all." The poem in this book grew out of that conversation. It was first published in the magazine *Mudfish* and later included in *Bite Every Sorrow*, Ras's first book, which won the Walt Whitman Award. C. K. Williams, in his judge's citation for the award, said, "Barbara Ras's ability to tap into the ordinary and draw forth profundity is brilliantly displayed in 'You Can't Have It All.'" Since then, the poem has happily enjoyed a life of its own.

About the Paintings

As reflected in the works that appear here, Terrell James's oeuvre expresses an intense interest in the "what" and "why" of places and how painting at the margins of awareness can reveal the truths available to art. Her study of subjects' light, color, and pictorial scales in relation to their objective actualities has unfolded in sites as diverse as Texas's vast Big Bend; Montauk, New York; coastal North Carolina; Beijing; and Berlin and reveals her practice and natural evolution as doppelgängers of each other. Forms continue to repeat throughout decades of painting in oil and acrylic. The hints of their interrelations, discovered as James's gestures emerge on canvas, multiply meanings for both artist and viewer. The narrative meaning of James's work is the record of the continual interpretation it spawns in memory and vision.

Images

PAGE II
Companion, 1997, acrylic and oil on board, 11¾ x 12¼ inches. Courtesy of the artist and Josh Pazda Hiram Butler Gallery, Houston. Photography by Thomas DuBrock

PAGE IV
The Game, 2015, acrylic on canvas, 66 × 66 inches. Collection of San Antonio Museum of Art, purchased with the Brown Foundation Contemporary Art Acquisition Fund. Photography by Ansen Seale

PAGE 2
Blades and Fins, 2021, oil on linen, 66 x 66 inches. Private collection, Houston. Photography by Thomas DuBrock

PAGE 4
At the End, 2015, oil and acrylic on canvas, 66 x 66 inches. Private collection, Dallas. Photography by Rick Wells

PAGE 8
Between Twins, 2018, oil on canvas, 42 x 42 inches. Private collection, London. Photography by Thomas DuBrock

PAGE 10
Shells on the Moon, 2018, oil on canvas, 66 x 66 inches. Private collection, London. Photography by Thomas DuBrock

PAGE 14
Shape Ranch 2, 2022, oil on canvas, 42 x 42 inches. Courtesy of the artist and Cadogan Gallery, London and Milan. Photography by Thomas DuBrock

PAGE 16
Long Tail, 2020, oil and mica on canvas, 42 x 42 inches. Private collection, Houston. Photography by Rick Wells

PAGE 18
A Talent for Friendship, 2018, oil on canvas, 42 x 42 inches. Private collection, London. Photography by Thomas DuBrock

PAGE 22
Acoustical Space, 2015, oil on canvas, 42 x 42 inches. Private collection, Houston. Photography by Thomas DuBrock

PAGE 24
Gone West, 2021, oil on linen, 66 x 66 inches. Private collection, London. Photography by Thomas DuBrock

PAGE 26
Rampart, 2016, oil on canvas, 66 x 66 inches. Private collection, Houston. Photography by Thomas DuBrock

PAGE 28
Three Mile Draw Revisited, 2021, oil on linen, 66 x 66 inches. Collection of the Modern Art Museum of Fort Worth. Photography by Thomas DuBrock

PAGE 30
Hover, 2013, oil on canvas, 66 x 66 inches. Courtesy of the artist and Barry Whistler Gallery, Dallas. Photography by Thomas DuBrock

Barbara Ras is the author of four poetry collections: *The Blues of Heaven*; *The Last Skin*, which was named the Texas Institute of Letters Best Book of 2010; *One Hidden Stuff*; and *Bite Every Sorrow*, which won the Walt Whitman Award and the Kate Tufts Discovery Award. She is also the editor of *Costa Rica: A Traveler's Literary Companion*, an anthology of short fiction in translation. She has received fellowships from the Guggenheim and Rockefeller foundations, among others, and has had residencies from the Bellagio Center, the Hermitage, Ucross Foundation, and the Vermont Studio Center. Ras has taught at the Warren Wilson MFA Program for Writers and other workshops nationally and internationally and has served as a Fulbright specialist at the University of the Western Cape in South Africa. For forty years she worked in book publishing, most recently as the founding director of the revitalized Trinity University Press. She lives in Denver.

Terrell James is a painter based in Houston. She has exhibited in China, Singapore, England, Italy, Germany, and Mexico since 2000 and is represented by galleries in Milan, Hong Kong, London, Houston, Dallas, and Portland, Oregon. Her work appears in the collections of the Whitney Museum of American Art; the Menil Collection; the National Gallery of Art; the Dallas Museum of Art; the Museum of Fine Arts Houston; the San Antonio Museum of Art; the Casa Lamm/Televisa Cultural Foundation and Museum, Mexico; the Museum of Fine Arts, Boston; and elsewhere. She has been an Edward F. Albee Foundation visual arts fellow, was named Texas Art League Houston's Texas Artist of the Year, and is the recipient of the Cultural Arts Council of Houston's Creative Artist Award. James worked for the Smithsonian Institution's Archives of American Art's Texas Project for five years and taught at the Museum of Fine Arts Houston's Glassell School for sixteen years.

Trinity University Press
San Antonio, Texas 78212

Book design by BookMatters, Berkeley
Photo of Barbara Ras by Anna Rucker
Photo of Terrell James by Wolf MacLean

Cover image: *Shape Ranch 2*, 2022, by Terrell James, courtesy of the artist and Cadogan Gallery, London and Milan, photographed by Thomas DuBrock

ISBN 978-1-59534-327-7 hardcover

Trinity University Press strives to produce its books using methods and materials in an environmentally sensitive manner. We favor working with manufacturers that practice sustainable management of all natural resources, produce paper using recycled stock, and manage forests with the best possible practices for people, biodiversity, and sustainability. The press is a member of the Green Press Initiative, a nonprofit program dedicated to supporting publishers in their efforts to reduce their impacts on endangered forests, climate change, and forest-dependent communities.

The paper used in this publication meets the minimum requirements of the American National Standard for Information Sciences—Permanence of Paper for Printed Library Materials, ANSI 39.48–1992.

Printed in Canada

CIP data on file at the Library of Congress

29 28 27 26 25 | 5 4 3 2 1